MORE THAN
90
MINUTES

Brighton & Hove Albion
1995 ~ 1997

TWO EXTRAORDINARY YEARS IN
THE LIFE OF A FOOTBALL CLUB

PHOTOGRAPHY & CAPTIONS: STEWART WEIR • TEXT: PAUL HAYWARD

ACKNOWLEDGEMENTS

FIRSTLY I would like to thank Adrian Wells of Detail Print. Without his belief in me this book would never have seen the light of a bookshelf. My wife Lorraine who had to cope with a photographer obsessed. Yiorgos Nikiteas who developed the black & white images you will see on the following pages. Paul Hayward of The Daily Telegraph who found the time to research and put into words what is a very complicated story. Paul Williams for the supply of the Leica M Camera which was used exclusively for the reportage of the season 96/97. Jackie Moores of Nikon for the loan of a variety of lenses to shoot the action over both seasons. Karen Buchanan at Four Four Two who ran several photo stories over the last two years. Kentmere for the supply of photographic material which was used for both the book and the More Than Ninety Minutes exhibition. Gordon Taylor at the PFA for its financial support. Gary Crittenden who set up the Albion internet web site and was responsible for allowing the world to see what was going on. Meridian and Sky TV for letting me into their studios. Bill, Jan and Anna Swallow, Attila the Stockbroker, Tim Carder, Gary O'Reilly and Hamish Crooks for their interest and input into this book. Liz Costa, Paul Samrah, The Vicar, Sarah Watts, Paul Whelch, Tony Foster, Warren Christmas, Ian Hart, Peter Kennard, Norman Rae, Paul Camillion, Mel and Kieron Moorman; just some of the many thousands of fans who battled and never gave up the fight. And not forgetting over 150 who were banned from the ground - particularly Simon Valder, The Coldean One.

Thanks of a kind are also due to Bill Archer for not responding to my calls or faxes and to David Bellotti for banning me once officially and once unofficially from the Goldstone. You didn't really think you could stop this book, did you? Thank you both for giving us - the fans - the worst days of our lives... and for what reason?

STEWART WEIR

Published by: More Than Ninety Minutes, Manor Barn, Poynings Road, Poynings, West Sussex BN45 7AG.

Designed and printed by Detail Print, Manor Barn, Poynings Road, Poynings, West Sussex BN45 7AG.

The views expressed in this book are not necessarily those of the publisher. Stronger words may be needed to fully describe the behaviour and activities of certain individuals.

ISBN - 0 9531214 0 2

CONTENTS

SPONSORED & SUPPORTED BY: Williams of Hove (Leica) • Brighton & Hove Council • Nikon UK • Detail Print • Kentmere Photographic • The PFA • Four Four Two Magazine • Brighton & Hove News

PREFACE

I WAS asked in early June 1995 if I would produce the action pictures for Albion's matchday programme by Tony Millard. I didn't hesitate to say yes. It occurred to me then that it would be an idea to produce a year-in-the-life photo documentary about the club. I put my ideas to chief executive David Bellotti and he agreed to give me access within the Goldstone.

A few weeks later the Brighton Evening Argus ran a story about the Goldstone being sold to developers. The club initially denied the story, then said it was true. The only problem was that the club had no replacement stadium and wanted the fans to travel to Portsmouth for all home games in the following season. So began the season of 1995/96.

I began supporting the Albion in the early 70s. I used to go with my dad, standing on a home-made box. I still had problems looking over everyone's shoulder to see the pitch. But at least there was a pitch to see.

The first game I remember watching was against Doncaster Rovers, who a quarter of a century later would be our opponents for the last game at the Goldstone.

The events that you will see unfold over the following pages should be seen for what they are: a disgrace to the name of British football. For the fans of the Seagulls this was a nightmare come true. For many people football is more powerful than any drug. It is an obsession. Was it any wonder that the fans would do everything they could to safeguard their heritage?

STEWART WEIR

WE WANT OUR BALL BACK!

HOW do you turn a diverse, easy-going bunch of south coast football fans into a seasoned, tightly-knit, organised and extremely angry pressure group with a taste for inventively-targeted direct action and the ability to take over the national media for weeks on end?

Well, what you do is this. You 'buy' their club for £56.25, install a politician with the hide of an armoured personnel carrier as your mouthpiece, sell their ground without a clue where the new one will be and call them 'half-brains' and 'troublemakers' as the club plunges, lemming-like, towards the abyss... Then you retire to your bolt-hole in Lancashire and sit back. And very soon, you won't know what hit you!

I don't think Bill Archer expected our response. I reckon he thought we were a bunch of stereotypically apathetic southerners who would just lie down and take it. How wrong can you be, eh, Bill? As things stand, we've won a partial but vital victory off the pitch and thanks to the Herculean efforts of Steve Gritt and his revitalised squad, a truly legendary one on it. The first week of May 1997 will long be remembered as one of the happiest of my life and the whole of this last season as an absolute nightmare - exhausting, frustrating, infuriating and yet ultimately exhilarating. And that on top of the previous season, which was hard enough...

This book stands as a testament to the ordinary Brighton fans' two year fight to save our club - to the way our common love of the Albion brought together people from all walks of life and united us in peaceful, inventive determination. As the moneymen seek to turn our game into their own personal playground, our message is quite simple. Profiteers, get out of football - it's our game, not theirs and what happened to our club should never, ever be allowed to happen again. FA, take action and fans, get organised. We want our ball back!

For me, the overriding inspiration during the past two years' bitter struggle has been the wonderful support we have had from football fans all over Britain - indeed, all over Europe - who realised we were fighting not just for Brighton and Hove Albion but for the grass roots of the game, for the soul of football in these days of Premier League stock exchange flotations and fifteen million pound transfers.

Fans United Day on February 8th was, quite simply, beautiful. To everybody involved in our campaign, everywhere - thanks, and well done. We've still got no ground and there are many battles ahead, but have no fear, one day soon, the Seagulls will soar again...

> "The battle's only just begun, but we have won the war.
> Our club, though torn asunder, will survive.
> And I salute each one of you who stood up, and said NO!
> and helped to keep the Albion alive.
> And one day, when our new home's built, and we are storming back
> A bunch of happy fans without a care
> We'll look back on our darkest hour, and raise our glasses high
> And say, with satisfaction: WE WERE THERE."

JOHN BAINE / ATTILA THE STOCKBROKER, FOUNDER, BRIGHTON INDEPENDENT SUPPORTERS' ASSOCIATION

The PROLOGUE

FALLING, FALLING. Every time you went the team got a little worse, the paint a little flakier and the sense of outrage - of the stupidity, the destructiveness of it all a little harder to bear. When did it start? With Gordon Smith's miss? When the money from the Lawrenson/Robinson/Ward transfers disappeared down Albion's bottomless hole of mismanagement? Wherever it started, Brighton supporters had a terrible, aching sense of where it would end. With a shopping centre on the Goldstone Ground and with the clock stopping on a century of football history.

Every day you woke feeling it couldn't get any worse, and it did. Every day you woke thinking the FA, the Government, the United Nations would send in the tanks. And they didn't. As the evidence unspooled the Brighton story spread like a fever down football's nervous system. It wasn't a little local difficulty, another example of a toy town board running a club into the ground through sheer incompetence. It was much broader than that. If you could do this to a football club - march in, sell the ground, waste the proceeds, break promises, let the team fall to the very gutter of the Football League... what message was being sent to every other club chairman? From 1993 you could sense the tumbleweeds coming to blow over the Goldstone. This was when they came. The three amigos... Archer, Stanley and Bellotti.

The period opened with the Seagulls at Wembley again, this time in a promotion play off with Notts County for a place in the old First Division, and ended with non-league Kingstonian knocking them out of the FA Cup first round. It began with Brighton scaring Liverpool at Anfield with a 2-2 draw in the 1990-91 FA Cup and ended with the club 16th in Division Two. In between Brighton were relegated from the old Division Two (1991-92) and crashed through the financial crisis of 1992-93 with Archer, Stanley and Bellotti in charge. Then, it looked like salvation, now it seems like the beginning of a slow and terrible illness.

The details: Brighton were at least £3m in debt and on the verge of extinction. On October 28 1993, with the club days away from being wound up in the High Court by the Inland Revenue, an emergency shareholders' meeting was called at the Grand Hotel. Those shareholders were told they must transfer their holdings to a 'shelf' company, Foray 585. (Dictionary term - Foray n. Sudden attack, raid.) Foray would repay the interest-free loans made by the directors, by June 10 1996.

The directors understood that the Co-op bank had agreed to offer a loan of £880,000 secured against the Goldstone and Stanley's personal assets. The Co-op may also have insisted that the other existing directors surrender their shares. But there is no record of the bank having laid down that condition. Greg Stanley was required to put up further collateral which would not be at risk as long as the value of the Goldstone (later to be set at £7.4m) exceeded the club's debts.

John Campbell, an Albion director who was communicating by fax from Nigeria states that his loan was listed as £50,000 when it should have been £105,000 (later corrected) and that the signature of a witness he had never met was added next to his own. In the meantime the crucial no-profit clause was removed from the club's constitution. That meant that if the club was wound up the shareholders were now free to profit from the sale of the Goldstone.

Bill Archer resident of Mellor, Blackburn, became the majority shareholder of Foray 585 and the most powerful figure on the board. His relationship with Stanley was as a partner in Focus DIY and trustee of the Stanley family's trust money. Archer's purchase of Brighton and Hove Albion FC cost just £56.25 and gave him a 56.25% majority shareholding. Greg Stanley's investment was £43.75, for which he received a 43.75% minority stake. Archer was in charge, for less than the price of an opera ticket.

SEASON 1995/96

THIS WAS the season when the veil fell away. "This isn't about football," a former player said, scanning the awful evidence. "This is about right and wrong." A life covering sport provides an intimate acquaintance with mendacity, yet few stories have horrified me like the sequence of events that began on July 7 1995, when the Argus broke the story that the Goldstone Ground had been sold, and that Brighton would play the following season at Portsmouth. The club had sold 93 years of history with no clear idea where they would go..

What follows will exert a kind of moral G Force on all who read it. In July 1995, when the stadium was sold, supporters were being promised a new 30,000-seat stadium (plus ice rink) at Waterhall just off the Brighton by-pass to the north. When the board advanced this fantastical promise, the local Council had already rejected plans for a retail development at Patcham Court Farm, from which the new ground was to be partly funded. In the same month, Greg Stanley resigned as chairman to be replaced by Archer; Bellotti claimed to be talking to Corals about a ground-share with the town's greyhounds, and the Football League restated a well-worn rule: that no club can enter a ground-share unless work is in progress for a new stadium in the club's home area.

Stranded amid this chaos was Liam Brady, Brighton manager and one of the finest midfielders to have played in Britain in the last 30 years. While Brady struggled to improve the team's prospects on a negligible transfer budget, it emerged in August that one of the club's Articles of Association had been altered. The old rule, which had been in place since 1903, had stated that in the event of the club being wound up shareholders would receive only their original investment - without profit. Any surplus would be donated to a charity or a sporting institution in Sussex. The change was made on November 23 1993, less than one month after Archer had taken control. When challenged, astonishingly, the club's solicitors claimed it was an "oversight" and promised to restore the original clause.

Also in August, Bellotti told supporters that the sale of the ground was essential to clear debts of £4.7m, a figure which has always been highly moveable. In his match day programme notes of September 2, Bellotti placed the debt at £6m. It was in that essay that he told supporters to "stop whining." The financial gymnastics were part of a long established pattern. As late as October 1996, Archer was still insisting in The Daily Telegraph that he and Stanley had injected £2m to save the club. In reality the Stanley Trust Loan had been in place since 1992, was secured on the Goldstone and was therefore not at risk. It was attracting interest of nearly £45,000 p.a. The May 1995 accounts revealed that the club would have to pay a further £250,000 as a penalty for not having paid the interest when due. To buy the club, Archer and Stanley spent £100. All other debts and loans would be repaid from the sale of the Goldstone. Revenue - £7.4m; Risk - Nil

And so to the time of the pitch invasions, of rage and bewilderment breaking the banks of the crumbling Goldstone terraces. They say people can take bad news as long as they know the truth. What was happening to Brighton was clouded in a fog of double talk and evasion. Those destroying the club, with the exception of Bellotti, who was Archer's dangling punch bag, were rarely seen at the ground, and seldom took the trouble to explain what was really happening. On September 2, a group of supporters occupied the centre circle and were persuaded by Brady to leave. Three weeks later during a live TV match against Bournemouth, supporters again took to the field. They were flailing in a darkness not of their making.

Falling, falling and faster. Late in September the FA finally stirred. Briefly. When the no-profit clause was removed, Archer had not informed Lancaster Gate and was thus in breach of FA regulations. As part of its investigation, the FA asked the Evening Argus to submit a file of evidence. Archer and Bellotti say they have never taken any money out of the club. "The club could not be in safer hands," wrote Bellotti on October 20. "Please trust us."

The Liam Brady era was drawing to a sad end. Brighton had attracted a leader who had played for Arsenal, Inter Milan and Juventus and was regarded as a manager of the utmost intelligence and integrity. In his time at Brighton he was able to spend just £15,000 on new players, and in November 1995 was unable to use a youth team minibus he had acquired after Bellotti refused to pay the cost of insurance. That premium was paid by supporters on November 18.

By now the Brighton story had descended into pathos, a dark Pythonesque comedy. On November 20, Brady resigned and was replaced by Jimmy Case. Soon after, Ivor Caplin, Leader of Hove Council, asked Stanley and Archer to stand down, and two days later demanded that the club finally open their accounts. The question asked was: do the board have something to hide? Stanley claimed to have resigned from the board on September 22 1995, but he and his wife were still listed at Companies House as directors.

A strange madness was setting in as Christmas approached. The club was imploding, a kind of wild comedy sweeping through the terraces and boardroom. Ivor Caplin was issued with a libel writ by Bellotti on behalf of Archer. Stanley's name was also on the document. Stanley later claimed to have no idea why he had been involved in such a serious legal action against a council official whose help was so badly needed by the club.

A closer look at the club accounts from this period revealed that the Stanley Trust loan of £600,000 had accrued interest of £381,000. Then, 16 days before Christmas, Fred Oliver, a 75 year old Argus paper seller, was escorted from the Goldstone and banned from selling the paper inside the ground. The Argus had carried a front-page story showing the extent of Stanley's potential profit on his loans to the club. Fred's dog, Bertie, was left tied up inside the ground while his owner was led out. Another day of shame.

Three days before Christmas, more fantasy from the boardroom. Bellotti called a press conference (the Evening Argus was not invited) to unveil a sports and retail complex at Toads Hole Valley. It was described by Steve Bassam, leader of Brighton Council, as "pie in the sky". Bellotti was still promoting the scheme on January 30 at a meeting with supporters groups, even though the Highways Agency and Hove Council had already rejected the idea.

The FA indicated that they wanted the board to put the proceeds from the ground sale into an independent account. This revealed two things - the FA's anxiety about where the remains of the £7.4m was going, and their inability or unwillingness to enforce their own rules. Bellotti said he had no intention of transferring the money into a 'transparent' account but would like to see all revenues coming into the club to go into a single account which the club would, of course, control.

In March, with planning permission assured, Chartwell offered the club a one-year lease back on the Goldstone for £480,000. Chartwell gave the club until 12 noon April 30 to sign the deal or vacate the ground. In April the board 'publicly' offered £200,000. Chartwell had already rejected this offer a week earlier. The FA asked the club why the deal had not been signed and why the board had not placed the proceeds from the sale of the ground into a transparent account. They asked the right questions but took no action.

On April 20 fans invaded the pitch again after a 1-0 victory over Carlisle. Supporters tried and failed to storm the directors' lounge so instead wrecked the directors' box and threw seat covers on to the pitch. Three days later, after a 2-1 defeat at Notts County, Brighton were relegated and the mood swung between despair and apoplexy. The following day a meeting between the board and brokers assembled by Brady went nowhere. The club made no announcement, offered no comfort. The last game at the Goldstone was to be on Saturday April 27.

On police advice, Bellotti agreed to miss the next home game. Albion supporters from across the footballing world converged on Hove. On the terraces, the talk was of demonstrating to the FA that the fans would not be ignored. A pitch invasion was inevitable. Only the timing was in question... Brighton v York was stopped at 3.16pm when at least 3,000 fans ran on to the pitch. At 3.34pm, with the goal posts wrecked, the match was abandoned. Not even the police were surprised. Bellotti was wise to stay away. The Brighton saga, worryingly, had crossed a line into chaos, even anarchy. Some Sunday newspapers reported it as a riot, with ominous implications for the staging of Euro 96.

The club was three days away from being ejected from the Goldstone, in trouble with the FA and in a state of unprecedented turmoil. People in other cities asked infuriatingly; what's going on at Brighton? Albion supporters offered a torrent of evidence and invective.

Hove Park, Sunday April 28, and Liam Brady emerges as a spokesman for the consortium. He tells a large crowd that the new grouping want to stay at the Goldstone and restructure the share issue, and asks Archer and Bellotti to resign. Brady also claims that Stanley is receptive to their ideas. He confirms that he will put £40,000 of his own money towards the deposit required to lease the Goldstone for another year. Bellotti treats the proposition with contempt: "The offer is totally irrelevant" and "the offer will not be accepted."

Tuesday April 30 was a day of high drama and high farce. Ten o'clock came and went without the promised statement about the leaseback deal. Around 40 minutes before the deadline, the board announced that the Goldstone would be rented for one final season. The cost of the deal was not announced. At 11.55, with people standing anxiously outside the ground, the contract was signed.

Bellotti, who had grappled with a photographer outside his house earlier that day, staged a bizarre press conference. Sitting in front of an empty trophy cabinet, he blamed the Argus for inciting the York 'riot' and sought credit for keeping the club at the Goldstone for one last season. He then asked Andy Naylor of the Argus to leave the room. Brighton had a home at least, but the money from the ground sale was draining fast, and the team were in the lowest division for the first time in 31 years. Supporters wondered when the board had decided they would sign the leaseback deal. Was it before the York game or later?

On this hinged the vital question of whether a near riot could have been averted.

It was a reprieve and another tragedy in one. Dragged this way and that, cold with anger and shock, Brighton supporters gathered their spirits for another long season of struggle.

The Goldstone has been sold although the news has not yet leaked out. Beneath the West Stand, pre-season training has started.

Summer training continues at Sussex University.

Palace score once, Albion not at all. Nigel Martyn saves. It's the last time Palace play at the Goldstone, the scene of many epic battles.

The annual August team photo. Paul McCarthy gets some grief for having a pose.

Fans return home from Albion's first away defeat at Peterborough. They didn't know it yet - things were going to get worse.

Stuart Tuck signs before leaving on the coach to Wrexham.

A peaceful half-time centre circle protest in the Notts County game. Liam Brady joins 200 fans to ask them to go back to the terraces. He says he understands their frustration. Meanwhile David Bellotti has Evening Argus photographer Simon Dack removed from the ground and in the match programme tells fans to "stop whining".

Albion win convincingly 1-0 at Bristol City. Liam Brady talks through the game with a local radio reporter.

Bill Archer, David Bellotti and Liam Brady talk in the Bristol City car park.

The Argus report on a challenge made by the joint Councils of Brighton and Hove to the club. The Councils say they would form a 'partnership' with the club if they withdraw from the sale of the Goldstone, abandon the Portsmouth ground-share and reinstate the 'no profit' clause.

A red card protest for the benefit of the thousands watching the Bournemouth away match live on TV.

As off-the-field developments unfurl, so do the banners. The board blame the Evening Argus for reporting what was happening; the supporters blame the board for making it happen in the first place.

Heads or tails? Steve Foster calls in the home match against Shrewsbury Town.

Following the joint council declaration to the club (18th September) Bill Archer emerges from three hours of talks with council representatives. He says that he would reveal at the end of the month a new stadium for the Albion. Money would also be available to Liam Brady to strengthen the squad.

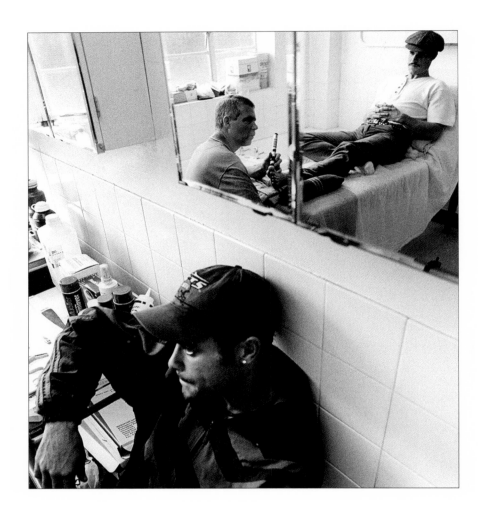

Sunday morning after the 3-1 home defeat v Swindon Town. Players come in for treatment. Jeff Minton waits as Stuart Storer gets some attention to his big toe from Physio Malcolm Stuart.

The frustrations of the sideline: Liam Brady shouts instructions - or possibly just shouts - during the game v Swansea City. Albion lose 0-2.

Leader of Hove Council, Ivor Caplin, tells 150 fans at a gathering at Southwick FC social club what he knows about the worsening situation.
Liam Brady attends but keeps a low profile.

A year after losing to Kingstonian, an FA Cup 1st round fixture at Canvey Island. Things are getting better: it's a 2-2 draw.

Jimmy Case follows Liam Brady up the tunnel after a 0-3 home loss to Walsall. Brady resigns the following day.

Jimmy Case gives his first interview as a manager. 7,000 fans forget about being second from bottom of Division 2 to watch Albion beat Canvey Island 4-1 in the FA Cup 1st round replay.

George Parris talks to David Bellotti about his contract in the York Forte Posthouse Hotel bar, before the York City game.

FA Cup 2nd round away to Fulham. The Junior Seagulls win a half-time shoot-out against Fulham Juniors. The first team draw 0-0.

FA Cup 2nd round replay against Fulham. As penalties beckon, Dean Wilkins replaces Stuart Myall in the last 10 minutes of extra-time.
Albion lose 1-4 on penalties.

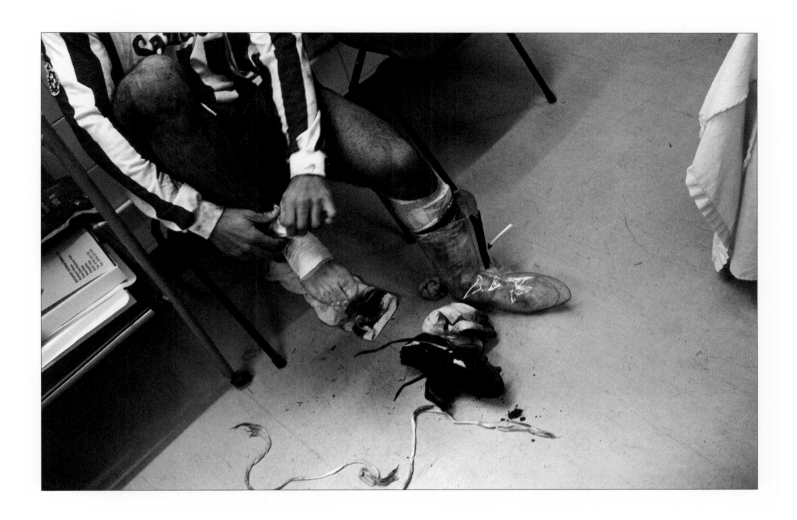

Happy New Year? Jeff Minton prepares for treatment on his ankle after the 1-1 home draw against Stockport County.

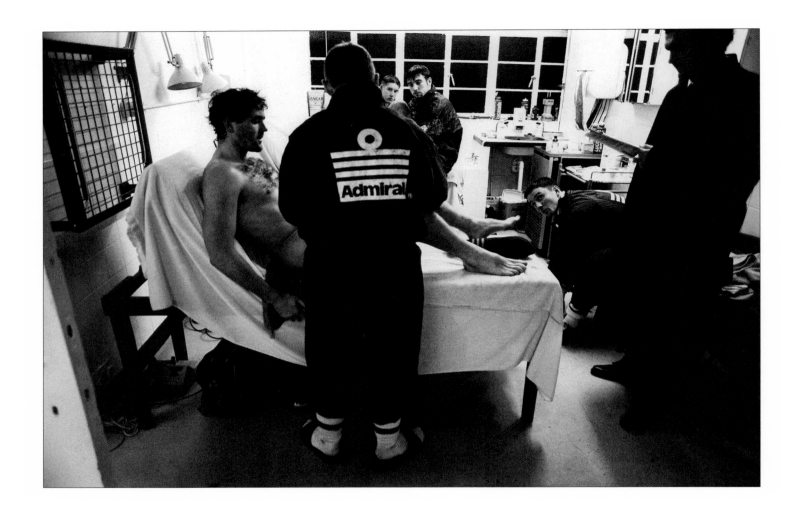

Another injury, another defeat. Paul McCarthy is treated for a groin strain after the 2-1 home defeat against Peterborough United.

Jimmy Case looks out of his dugout. It's a bore draw on a drab Tuesday night in Hull.

A new stadium at Toads Hole Valley? Hove Council says no. The Highways Agency says no. The fans say we don't believe you and where's the money coming from? David Bellotti explains the club's 30,000 all-seater multi-purpose stadium complete with a lot of bright colours and promises.

So nearly: Albion supporters react to a dipping 25-yard shot from Stuart Myall minutes before the end of a 1-1 draw at Oxford United.

The classic cliché. Father and son watch as Albion lose 0-2 at home to Bristol City.

After the match, fans try to get into the West Stand to confront David Bellotti. Things were starting to get nasty. Bellotti continued to take no notice of the supporters and many of them felt that direct action was the only way of expressing their views.

Mascots wait in the corridor for the players to come out for the game against Brentford. It was to be goalless.

On the training pitch.

Junior McDougald contemplates and Nicky Rust tells Jeff Minton a story on the pitch before the game against Chesterfield.

Forgotten joy as Albion thrash Hull City 4-0. It's the first home win since December 9.

2.35pm at home to Rotherham United. The view from the players' tunnel. Albion are second from bottom and five points from safety.

Albion have lost the previous two away games. The West Stand watch as Burnley lose 1-0.

Albion v Carlisle United. Referee Steve Bennett and assistants Tingy and Torrance relax in their changing room. With three games to go, staying in the Second Division is no more than a distant possibility. Carlisle are six points ahead but very much involved in the dog fight. Albion need to win all their remaining games and rely on Swansea losing theirs.

George Parris talks to Carlisle goalkeeper Tony Caig minutes before they run out on to the pitch.

An early bath for Jeff Minton, sent off after a dispute with ex-Albion triallist Warren Aspinall.

Albion win 1-0 but the fans' fury is overwhelming. All they want to do is get their hands on David Bellotti.

Supporters make it to the doors of the Directors' Lounge. As the doors are kicked and the glass is broken, the Directors' seats are ripped out and the covers are thrown on the pitch.

Order is restored.

Around 300 fans gather in the Concorde Bar. Another 250 are locked outside. Greg Stanley says, "I am giving my commitment. We are staying at the Goldstone whatever it costs. My word is my honour." Stanley claims there is a consortium willing to invest in the club, but only if Archer and Bellotti go. He says, "We have got to meet the people this week." Meanwhile the team must win tomorrow night at Notts County to stand a chance of staying up.

Three days have passed since Notts County won 2-1 at home and the Albion were relegated into the Third Division. Groundsman Brian Harwood mows in front of the North Stand, it seems for the last time.

Albion v York City "Before the game I said to my wife: 'I'm going to be home late tonight, because something is going to happen after the game. I was standing on the old East Terrace, God I love it, with my brother. It all went off after quarter of an hour and my brother said: 'this game isn't going to finish, so if we want to be a part of this we're going now.' So we went down there then. I don't mind telling you, we got down on to the pitch and I was crying my eyes out because it was the last time I was ever - I'm doing it again - it was the last time I was ever going to be there." Nigel Summers

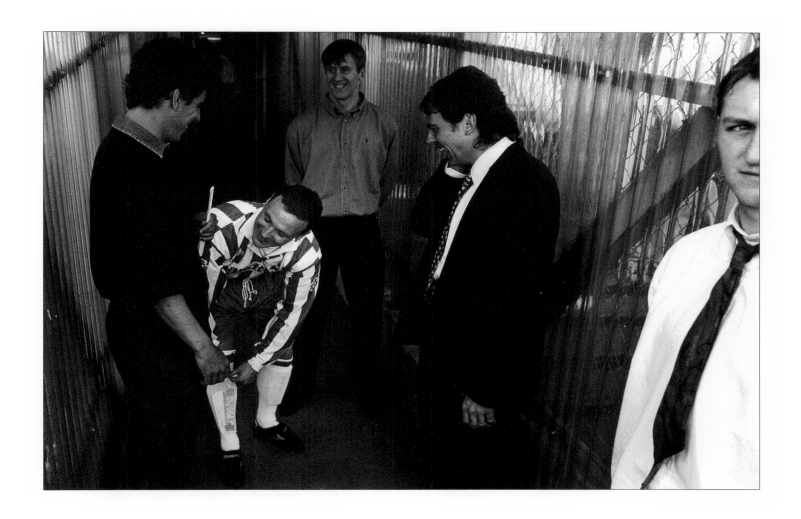

Ian Chapman waits in the tunnel before receiving his Player of the Year award. Ironically, Jimmy Case had already decided that Chapman no longer figured in his plans for next season in Division Three.

At 3.16pm at least 3,000 fans run on to the pitch. Players and officials run off it for cover.

The players' tunnel is wrecked in a show of frustration and hate at the way the club is being run.

Standing on the home dugout, fans vent their fury at an empty directors' box.

Souvenirs of turf that has seen 94 years of studs from Liverpool to Leatherhead.

The police regain control. The pitch is clear of supporters, although signs of earlier protests remain.

A view of the South goal through gate 15. The events of yesterday are splashed on the front pages of every national newspaper and reported worldwide. The Brighton situation is now the talking point among football supporters everywhere.

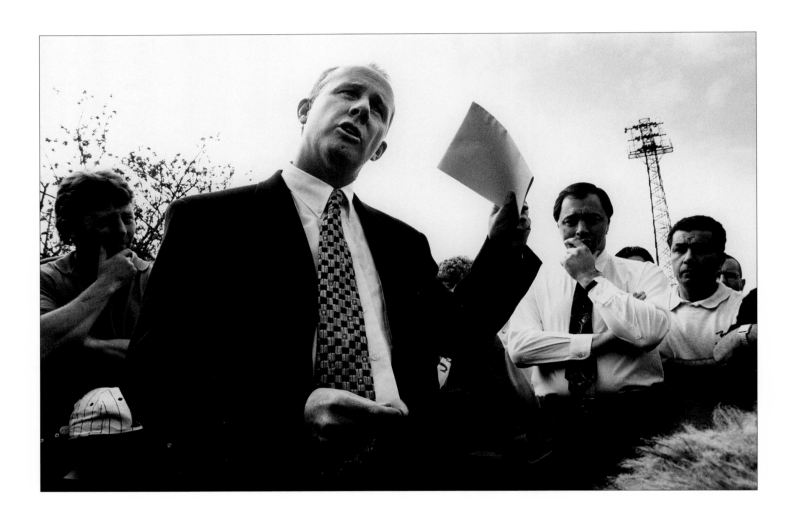

At 11am on Sunday morning in Hove Park, Liam Brady emerges as a spokesman for the consortium wanting to take control of the Albion. He says that the consortium will put new money into the club and believes that with good administration and PR, the club can attract sponsorship and work with the council to get a new stadium. He asks for Archer and Bellotti to resign. Greg Stanley had been receptive; Bill Archer had not.

10.15am... waiting, waiting, waiting. This was the day of judgement. In March the Goldstone's new owners, Chartwell, had given the club until mid-day on April 30 to either agree to a £480,000 leaseback of the ground or vacate it. The board offered £200,000 and said that was it: take it or we'll go to Portsmouth. We will probably never know Archer's motives for refusing to sign an agreement before the last home game of the season on April 27 but it was a refusal that made the disturbances inevitable. On the following Tuesday - deadline day - the club promised a statement by 10am. As fans gather opposite the Goldstone in Hove Park on a sunny spring morning no one knows which way the decision will go.

At 11.03 Paul Samrah (centre) and Nigel Summers (right) react as news comes through that the deal has been done. The club will stay at the Goldstone for one last season.

Greg Stanley gives his views to the media.

In front of an empty trophy cabinet David Bellotti asks for credit in keeping the club at the Goldstone for one last season. He blames the Brighton Evening Argus for inciting the York 'riot' and then tells Argus reporter Andy Naylor to leave the room.

Albion's reputation goes before them. The police take no chances as they line up in front of the Brighton fans at the end of the season's final away match, at Walsall. The result is irrelevant.

In a show of footballing solidarity, Walsall fans celebrate the end of their season by singing in support of Brighton. Their gesture is reciprocated; shirts are swapped.

In front of a crowd of 2,106 on a Thursday morning, the match against York City is resumed. Results on Saturday mean that York City must win to avoid the drop at Carlisle United's expense. Carlisle Chairman Michael Knighton is naturally delighted as Craig Maskell puts Albion ahead.

York fans can't believe an open goal is missed.

Saved from the drop. It's 3-1 to York. Carlisle are relegated with Brighton, Swansea and Hull City.

York players return in joy to their changing room.

Season 1995-96 ends. Events off the pitch undoubtedly had their effect on it. For the first time since 1965 the Seagulls will play the following season in the basement division. What the supporters couldn't predict was the creation of no-go zones and the banning of non-season ticket holders from every stand except the North, all for the protection of David Bellotti, officer in charge of Fortress Goldstone.

SEASON 1996/97

NINE months left. Maybe. The terraces simmering and the clock ticking towards Albion's doom. It began against Chester City on August 17 and might have ended at home to Doncaster the following April. It was the year that Brighton supporters told the rest of British football: this is about More Than Ninety Minutes.

It was a year of laughter in the dark, with an unlikely, light-splashed end with the glories of Edgar Street, Hereford, on May 3. But few really expected the Albion to survive. Bellotti set the tone for the season as early as June of '96. He raised ticket prices for the terraces and the South Stand seats by 15% but left the West Stand alone. In July, Archer again confirmed that he would step aside if his famous three criteria were met. (He had asked the consortium: what sort of expertise had they got to be able to build a stadium, what funds were there for its construction and could they "deliver the future"?)

What followed was a landslide of pain and acrimony. On August 16 the FA ruled that the club had been found guilty of 'failing to control a crowd' at the York City match on April 27, and laid down a suspended three-point deduction. They ruled that one game would have to be played behind closed doors if there were any further incursions on to the pitch.

On August 21, Archer wrote to Paul Samrah, chartered accountant, Gulls Eye writer and heroically persistent advocate of the supporters' struggle. "After my meeting with the consortium," wrote Archer in typically ungrammatical mode, "I will arrange a meeting for the Supporter Club Executives (sic) to here (sic) the financial package. My intention is for the supporters to decide. It is a very important time in the Clubs (sic) history to get this right. The current owners have the desire to develop a new stadium, but without the support, I am not going to attempt to push water uphill... That's why ultimately you and the Supporters Club Members will decide!"

The letter was a classic Archerism. Of Bellotti, he wrote: "His profile in future will be zero comment. I will be making the statements, hopefully after consultation with the supporters. I have the bit between my teeth to deliver a new stadium, but will go if it is proven that anyone else can deliver the new stadium and a cash flow to build a strong team."

Looking back it is enough to make you weep. Bellotti kept on talking all right, and Archer's voice was seldom heard. Nor was his face seen. By September postcards showing Archer with "Demon Eyes" and asking him to go were flooding into his home.

In October the mood darkened again. Against Lincoln City, fans invaded the pitch to stage a peaceful sit down protest. The game was held up for 13 minutes. The following weekend a delegation travelled up to Mellor to demonstrate outside Archer's house after Brighton played Wigan. Some stayed on to protest outside the Blackburn branch of Focus DIY. By now Albion supporters were attracting support and encouragement across the land. A template was being created for future resistance struggles.

On the airwaves and in the press, more acrimony flowed. On October 4, on BBC South Today, Archer said: "I haven't been convinced that they (the consortium) have the funds to build a new stadium." The consortium insisted that they had supplied documentary proof of their funding resources both to Archer and the FA. If so, the three preconditions had been met and Archer should have moved aside. From the same interview: "If anyone can demonstrate they can build a stadium better than me, and they have more funds to build a new stadium better than me, then I will genuinely step aside."

Archer had no approved site and no obvious source of funding. The club were losing an estimated £1m a season and the team were bottom of the league's 92 clubs and in freefall. Between September 7 and the end of October 29, they lost nine games out of twelve. In any other industry, the board would have been forced to resign for incompetence alone.

Also in October, Stewart Weir, the creator of this book, was banned from the Goldstone until Boxing Day. An "unofficial" ban was then enforced until late February after he was spotted outside Bellotti's house with other supporters. Bellotti, the former Liberal Democrat MP, whose party is rooted in the principle of free speech and open debate, was attempting to crush dissent and drive his opponents from the ground.

Fans without season tickets were confined to the North Stand. Bellotti was determined to see every home game, whatever the consequences. Jimmy Case pleaded with him not to attend matches because his presence was exacerbating the team's problems. The eyes and voices of supporters were trained not on the pitch but on the directors' box. Again and again Bellotti refused to stay away. His intention was to show himself in control. He sat, cold-faced, under an avalanche of loathing and abuse. The Goldstone Ground went Soviet.

On October 10, Archer said on Radio Five Live: "Myself and Greg Stanley took the decision that we would bail the club out... we had to inject another £2m to keep the club afloat." In 1993, when Archer and Stanley took control, the only hard cash invested was an £880,000 bank loan secured on the Goldstone Ground. Archer invested £56.25. It wasn't a financial masterstroke. A schoolboy could have saved the club by selling the ground to pay off the debts.

Six days earlier, Archer had said: "There was 10 million quid's worth of rolled up losses." The debts of Brighton and Hove Albion FC have never been that high. In the same interview, Archer said: "I have been watching Brighton and Hove Albion for the last eight years." This was news to the regulars in the West Stand.

Against Hereford on October 15, supporters walked out 15 minutes before the end. On October 28 a fans' forum at Hove Town Hall was addressed by Dick Knight. You could smell the sulphur, the rage building up. After a long debate, a vote was passed unanimously to stage a complete boycott against Mansfield Town on November 9. The following day a petition bearing 6,500 signatures was presented at the head office of Focus DIY in Crewe. In the bars of Sussex, there was talk of serious public disorder and injury or even death. Tense, scary times, with no progress and hope dissolving fast.

On November 9, Bellotti, who had supposedly been gagged by Archer, gave a long interview to South Coast Radio in which he said: "The Football Association have no authority in this matter." Bellotti also insisted: "There isn't any possibility whatsoever that Mr Knight will be a part in the future of Brighton and Hove Albion Football Club..."

November was a desperate month, a freak show that defied the constant claim that things could get no worse. On Saturday November 9 came a show of defiance and solidarity. A boycott of the Mansfield match reduced the official attendance to 1,933. The real figure was closer to 800, which included 400 visitors from Mansfield. The higher figure took into account absent season ticket holders. Around 2,000 fans stayed outside until minutes before the end of the first-half, when nearly a thousand came through an "unlocked" gate on to the East Terrace. At half-time supporters of both teams poured on to the pitch and then breached the exclusion zone Bellotti had created in the West Stand. The chief executive was not seen again that day.

The Daily Telegraph asked Chartwell Land for a categoric assurance that no monies above the published £7.4m were payable for the Goldstone Ground. They replied: "No further sums are due to the Club or bodies associated with the Club."

And down, down the Seagulls went. In late November, Michael Standing, an England schoolboy and the club's most talented youngster, admitted that he was considering offers from other clubs. "There's no way I can carry on the way it is," he said. On the night of Tuesday November 26, the bottom of the pit was reached. Brighton lost at home 4-3 on penalties to Sudbury Town in the FA Cup first-round. It was the second time in three seasons Brighton had been eliminated by non-league opposition. In the Argus, Steve Foster said: "There is no ambition off the pitch and sadly there is none on it either."

Gary Stevens, one of the finest players to have passed through the club, said: "After 90 minutes I expected to see him (Jimmy Case) getting hold of someone by the throat and giving the players a kick up the backside. There did not seem to be any animation. But if he was to be sacked or wanted to resign afterwards there wasn't a board member there to deal with it anyway."

On November 28, Graham Kelly issued an open letter to Archer urging him to enter talks organised by the Centre for Dispute Resolution, an offshoot of the CBI. The FA, who had been urged to charge the Archer regime for alleged misconduct but preferred to pass the case sideways, would meet the cost of the mediation. Twenty-four hours later Archer announced that Brighton would ground-share with Gillingham for the next two seasons. A family trip to Gillingham (a two hour drive) would cost more than Archer's £56.25 investment. The FA were said to be incensed that Archer had chosen the following day to issue such a provocative statement.

One day after that, on the Saturday, supporters assembled at Victoria for a march to Marble Arch and rally in Hyde Park. A petition was handed in at FA headquarters at Lancaster Gate. It contained 5,726 signatures. The campaign to save the club had grown to epic proportions.

The pace of events was dizzying. Against Darlington on December 3, Bellotti was chased from the ground after arriving in the directors' box three minutes after kick-off. The biggest visual indictment of the board was empty directors' seats: the best in the house, vacant, the ultimate symbol of Brighton's shame. The team were nine points adrift at the bottom and the following day Jimmy Case was sacked. Dennis Rofe (ex-coach at Southampton), Glenn Roeder and Dave Merrington were mentioned as possible successors. Nobody thought of Steve Gritt. On the same day, Liam Brady, now director of youth football at Arsenal, said: "Jimmy has been in a diabolical position to work for these people. They have made an absolute mockery of the club."

It got worse. We were in a maelstrom. While the back pages analysed the fall of Case, the Argus led the front with the news that Brighton were "flat broke." Accounts filed at Companies House showed that Brighton had made a trading loss of £1m in the previous financial year. The figures showed a drop in gate receipts of 19% and a fall in other income (sponsorship etc.) of 47%. With a possible capital gains tax bill of £1.3m pending, the club had almost certainly spent the £7.4m from the ground sale on debt repayment.

The previous month, Archer had said: "The club is now solvent. Our last balance sheet shows that we've gone from something like minus £900,000 to £500,000 profit, so we've actually turned it round." On December 9, the FA implemented part of the suspended sanction imposed on the club in the wake of the York City match. The disciplinary committee deducted two points as punishment for the pitch invasion in the Lincoln game. It might have been three, with an order to play one game behind closed doors. Brighton fell 11 points behind.

On December 10, I interviewed Greg Stanley for my newspaper. He said: "I've been supporting this consortium from day one. That is a fact." Of the Archer - Bellotti regime, which many fans argued only Stanley had the power to depose, he said: "It's over, it's finished, and something terrible is going to happen. Somebody is going to get hurt. Enough is enough. It's got to be handed over and let the consortium build the new stadium." On the same day, Knight was interviewed on Newsnight, which made the familiar error of suggesting that Brighton were merely victims in the growing gulf between rich and poor.

Every day brought fresh news. On December 11 Gritt was appointed manager and Merrington, who had been interviewed, castigated the club for not telling him in person that he hadn't got the the job. Merrington said he was told of Gritt's appointment by the media. The papers were unanimous. Gritt had just taken the worst job in football. For his first game in charge, where one thousand whistles and balloons (sponsored by McAlpine) were released, he was vilified as a 'puppet' by some sections of the crowd. But Brighton beat Hull 3-0, a miracle of sorts.

Before Christmas, a vital intervention was made by the barrister and expert on Sport and the Law, Edward Grayson, who argued that the FA was in breach of its own constitution in not charging the board under rule 26, which deals with "misconduct or any matter which, in the opinion of the Council, is considered to be... improper behaviour or likely to bring the game into disrepute." Grayson argued that there were numerous precedents for the FA pursuing such actions, and was a constant friend to Brighton supporters.

The festive spirit was running free at the Goldstone. Five days before Christmas, Bellotti wrote to Paul Samrah banning him from the ground until the end of the following season (ie 20 months). "You have been seen to leave your seat to lead protests and threats at the Directors' Box," wrote Bellotti. Samrah, not surprisingly, consulted his solicitors. The goodwill spilled over into the New Year. In January, the Latest magazine ran an interview with Stanley, quoting him as saying, of Bellotti: "I cannot stand the bloke. I can't stick listening to his whining all the time. His PR is appalling and it's outrageous the amount of money that is spent on extra police and stewards to protect him."

On January 17, a meeting with Edward Grayson was held at the Oak Hotel. Grayson outlined how Brighton supporters could pursue legal action against the FA for failing to apply their own rules. A solicitor was appointed, but supporters' groups deferred litigation until after the results of the mediation were known. Meanwhile, Bellotti wrote two bouncing cheques for £250 each to Lifeline lottery winners. He called it 'an oversight' and promised to honour the cheques.

The pace of events slowed until early February, when a landmark in British football history was laid with Fans United day. The idea came from Richard Vaughn, a Plymouth Argyle supporter, via the internet. He suggested that a day be set aside for football fans to visit the Goldstone and pledge support for Albion supporters. They would also express their disgust at the way Archer was running the club. It was a day to make your heart both soar and weep. After messages of support had gushed in from around the world on the internet, thousands of supporters from all over Britain and Europe (plus a few exiled Albion fans from Singapore, New York and Washington) came to Brighton and Hove, many wearing their own club shirts. It was a festival of defiance which inspired the players to a 5-0 win over Hartlepool. It was an anaesthetic to all the pain of the preceding months. The following day, the ache and the tears were back.

A TV studio in Southampton, Sunday February 9. The consortium have declined to attend, citing the confidentiality clause in the mediation process, but Archer is present on a satellite link and Bellotti is in the studio, protected by police dogs. With wonderful symbolism, Archer has a patch over one eye.

The programme is a travesty. Archer and Bellotti take charge, none of the big questions are asked and the fans are corralled by dogs into the hospitality room. In a pre-recorded interview, Graham Kelly says: "Brighton and Hove Albion aren't the only club with problems at the present time. We have an enormous number of football clubs to look after under our jurisdiction and we can't take special action in respect of one out of 42,000 clubs."

While form improved, the talks were conducted in strict secrecy, with constant postponements and problems. Bellotti was deselected as a county councillor for Eastbourne Park Ward and Grayson came up with an interesting cutting from 1984. It concerned the banning of Anton Johnson, former chairman of Rotherham and Southend, for his part in "a very grubby affair". The presiding Football League official was Graham Kelly.

Albion supporters were going down the long slide to oblivion with two flimsy hopes: that the Knight consortium would save the club and that the team would extract themselves from their dungeon. Their only joy was a succession of thrilling home victories. The team were stirring. The gap between 91st and 92nd place was narrowing. Steve Gritt was trading in wonders.

Players prepare for the last Goldstone photocall.

Good start for the North Stand: the first game is a 2-1 win against Chester City.

After the Coca Cola Cup 1st round game against Birmingham City, North Standers have a sit-in and are eventually removed.

Gary Hobson and Jason Peake leave Ninian Park, Cardiff, dejected after a 1-0 defeat.

Supporters thought Barnet would be a walkover. Goal to the home side as they win 3-0.

Noel Cook from Lewes shows off his new t-shirt before the game against Scunthorpe United. It ends 1-1.

George Parris whips one in against Scarborough. By this time the left side of the players' tunnel is a no-go zone. It's not long before the right side suffers the same fate. The Bellottis are just visible above Parris's left shoulder in an otherwise vacant directors' box. Albion win 3-2.

Away to Colchester. Having seen a goal conceded only minutes earlier, Albion fans wait for another free kick against them just outside the penalty area. Colchester win 2-0.

Early morning breakfast on the way to Exeter, in another motorway service station. Exeter win 2-1.

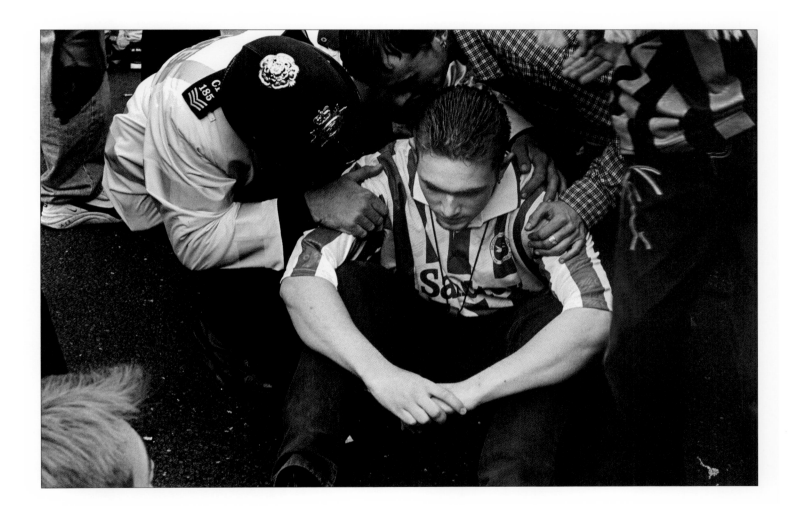

After a 2-2 draw at home against Torquay United, the first of many sit-down protests outside the main West Stand. Fans are getting increasingly frustrated with Archer's attitude and Bellotti's apparent ineptitude.

The Liberal Democrat conference comes to town. As David Bellotti is one of their councillors, fans air their views to anyone who will listen. As a result the Lib Dems lose the front cover of the Argus to the fans. Mr Ashdown is said to be very annoyed.

Liberal Democrat Clive Gray (right) talks to Tony Foster at a meeting of the supporters' club. Gray said he would ask Bellotti to resign, but was never heard of again.

Outside Northampton Town's new Sixfields stadium. A smart ground to visit but it didn't make up for a 3-0 thrashing.

Sunday morning at Sky TV. Liz Costa (second right) spreads the gospel about what can happen when dictators rather than directors run a football club.

At Lancaster Gate Dick Knight feels the frustration of dealing with the FA and the club board.

Steve Double (background) reflects as Graham Kelly explains that the FA is doing all it can to solve the problem. Meanwhile, Bill Archer and David Bellotti are leaving through a back door to avoid both fans and press. The day ends as it began. No progress.

Tensions running high. Archer announced before the home game against Lincoln that the club would not be talking to the consortium again. During the game around 100 fans run on to the pitch to voice their anger at both the FA and the club. The match is held up for 13 minutes. The three-points deduction suspended from the York City match could now be applied.

In the Guardian's Soccer Diary today: "Apparently, Brighton chairman Bill Archer reckons Seagull supporters' fears about the club's future are groundless." Meanwhile, after the loss at Wigan, around 200 fans march through Archer's home village of Mellor, Lancashire to tell him that he isn't wanted.

Build a bonfire... Build a bonfire. Archer isn't at home.

Banned. For the first time I get a view from the outside, as Cambridge win 2-1. Leaflets are distributed calling for a walk-out 15 minutes before the end of the match against Hereford. The signal for the exodus will be unmistakable.

As Chinese sky bombs explode, 2,000 fans walk out of the game against Hereford United with 15 minutes to play. A sense of togetherness, camaraderie and the will to win was developing among supporters. The team lose 1-0.

After visiting Bellotti's house the previous night, these fans were told that he would see them and talk about the problems. Bellotti didn't turn up after three hours of waiting. It appears he went to Gillingham to talk to their chairman, Paul Scally.

Doncaster is not the most pleasant of grounds to watch your team crash 3-0, a 15th consecutive away defeat.

Before the game against Fulham, Albion and Fulham fans march from Brighton Station to the Goldstone.

A meeting of fans at Hove Town Hall. Up for discussion is what to do next in the developing war of attrition. By this time many fans were being banned from the Goldstone. Supporters debate the pros and cons of a total boycott of either one game or several. Depriving income into the club would make a much-needed point to Archer.

A unanimous vote to boycott the Mansfield Town match. Graham Talbot, who hadn't missed a match home or away since 1970 (1,342 games), said even he wouldn't go in.

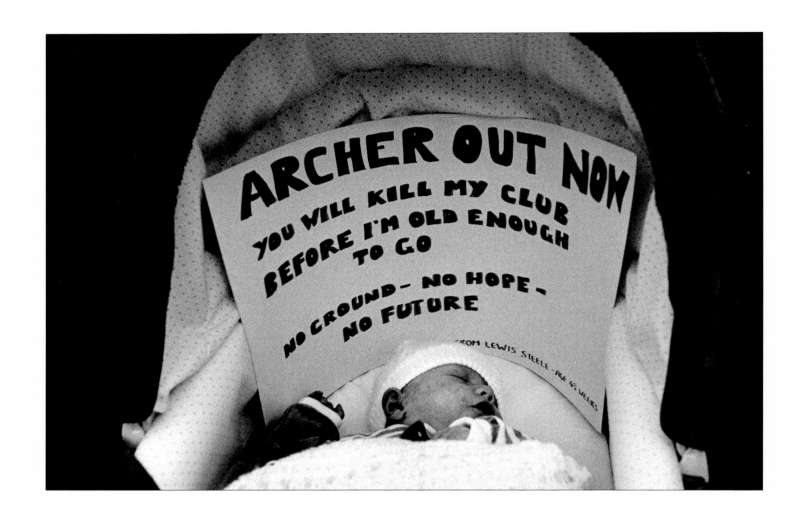

On the way to Rochdale, supporters visit Bill Archer's Focus DIY head office in Crewe. The doors were locked and a petition of 6,500 names is left outside the front entrance. Mr Archer isn't there to take stock of the growing hate and distrust.

In the dying minutes of the match against Hartlepool United, Albion are 3-2 up. Jimmy Case touches wood as Hartlepool get their last chance to draw. It's the first away win since March 6.

"The ultimate measure of a man is not where he stands in moments of comfort and convenience but where he stands at times of challenge and controversy" (Martin Luther King). Boycott day has arrived. Home against Mansfield Town. A day of reckoning, it would either be an embarrassing flop or it would show the football world where the Brighton fans were prepared to stand.

Fan against fan was a recipe for conflict within. It is forceful but not nasty.

The organisers had asked simply that fans stay away, but around 1,500 gather outside the North Stand as the match begins.

At 3.40pm gate 15 mysteriously opens. 1,000 fans pour in. At half-time Brighton fans meet Mansfield fans on the pitch. The police and stewards just look the other way. David Bellotti is not seen again that day.

The Mansfield supporters' view from the South East. Albion and Mansfield fans take back the Bellotti-imposed no-go zones.

After a penalty is given and scored, Brighton fans go crazy. The result is a 1-1 draw.

At the end of the day Bill Archer's effigy is burned in Hove Park. The day is a success. The official attendance is 1,933. This figure includes all season ticket holders and the Mansfield contingent. A rough head count suggests a true figure closer to 800, including 400 visitors from Mansfield. A steward later says that only 88 paid to go into the North Stand.

The embarrassment of a possible early exit from the FA Cup 1st round against non-league Sudbury Town. The media write about a 0-0 draw.
Not quite a shock but it's good enough. "Sudbury will get stuffed 5-0 at our place," says a Brighton fan on the way back to his car.

Fifty eight Albion fans make the mid-week trip to Swansea. Another home attack narrowly fails.

Sudbury Town 1 - Brighton and Hove Albion 1. After extra time it goes to penalties. If ever there is a low point in a football league club's season it's going out to a non-league club. Sudbury score to win 4-3. The Goldstone becomes a playground for Sudbury fans.
The press have a story.

Can things really get worse than this? The North Stand in shock. Motionless and disbelieving.

A visit to Fulham is a perfect excuse to march from Victoria Station to Hyde Park.

A petition of 5,726 names for the FA.

Things are starting to get scary. Two minutes into the match against Darlington, around 70 fans vacate the North Stand to get their hands on David Bellotti. He runs for safety. Darlington win 3-2 and at the end of the game 200 fans try to break into the East Terrace (above). Windows in the West Stand are smashed. The match stewards vote to walk out if Bellotti ever turns up for a home match again. It was a watershed in the struggle to improve everything on the pitch and off it. Jimmy Case was sacked the following day.

The team are managerless as Ian Baird has a fitness test. The club accounts covering the period up to May 31 1996 reveal that if all debts were paid off, the club would have only around £450,000 left. Losses per month are around £76,000.

With no game on, a group of fans travel back up to Mellor to try to reason with Bill Archer. Attila the Stockbroker writes a letter to him somewhere on the M6. Archer isn't in but the police are. The letter is hand-delivered anyway.

The FA's Steve Double leaves the Goldstone. The Lincoln City pitch demonstration prompted the FA to send its disciplinary committee into action. Later this afternoon two points were to be deducted from the Albion's meagre tally of 13 from 22 games, making the gap between 91st and 92nd club 11 points. The Albion had also played more games than many of their rivals. The FA had finally swung into action.

No one expected Steve Gritt to be announced as manager. He had taken on both the worst and the hardest job in football. Did he check the club's position before he said yes? With past glories on the wall was he going to be able to pull it off... the greatest escape of them all?

Gritt is greeted with boos from the crowd. It was nothing personal. Just a message to Archer. Hull are the day's visitors. 1,000 balloons in blue, white, gold and black (the two teams' colours) are released over the Goldstone. Whistles are also given out to create confusion for the referee. All they do is to create a 'San Siro' atmosphere. The furthest balloon reaches Montpellier, France.

At half-time Ian Taylor handcuffs himself to the goal. Later in court he says he had hoped to handcuff himself to Bellotti. "I made this non-violent form of protest out of desperation." He was banned for three months. The day finishes with a 3-0 win over Hull: the first home victory since Scarborough in September. Gritt starts with a 100 per-cent home record.

The game against Fulham in the Auto Windscreens Shield is played. Only 1,384 see a thriller game go into extra time after both teams score two each. Nicky Rust goes wild as the Albion win 3-2 with 'the golden goal'.

Training at Sussex University. Steve Gritt goes through the game plan before travelling up to Orient.

Peter Shilton's 1,000th game is watched by millions on Sky TV. Albion go camera shy and lose 2-0. At the end of the game Albion fans have another sit-in. A Southend United fan shows a bit of solidarity and is dragged outside for his trouble.

Happy New Year? An away day to Torquay. The coach breaks down at a service station on the M27. Fans push 12 tons uphill - a suitable metaphor for their season so far.

A long way home after losing 2-1.

Today's game at home to Northampton is called off. Fans visit Bellotti's house and throw a few snowballs.

Steve Gritt and Jeff Wood meet fans at the Concorde Bar. They get a good reception.

Edward Grayson, the country's leading expert on law and sport, meets supporters' representatives. He says he is convinced that the FA have the power to remove the current directors from football management if found guilty of misconduct. He also said that, to protect the game from abuse, it is the FA's duty to charge them.

Gritt and Wood celebrate as Stuart Storer scores with a flying header to make it 1-1. In the 89th minute Lincoln City score to win the game.

The banned celebrate from an overlooking garden as Albion go 2-0 up against Rochdale. The match eventually ends 3-0. In a survey before the game 1,328 fans are asked: "do you intend to watch the Albion at Gillingham regularly under the present owners?". Five per cent say yes. When asked: "would you be more inclined to watch the Albion at Gillingham if the consortium took over?", 69 per cent say yes.

The previous day the Centre for Dispute Resolution released a statement of progress. "The framework for a potential restructuring of the club was pursued and some further progress was made," etc. Today in CEDR's offices supporters' groups meet Bill Archer. David Bellotti is kept outside for seven hours. Three concessions are won: Bellotti will not appear at home games; areas presently restricted to season ticket holders will be re-opened (except the West Stand seats) and Paul Samrah will have his Goldstone ban lifted.

The Albion dugout can't believe a goal is missed. It's a 1-1 draw at Mansfield.

The February 8th idea is a truly beautiful one and I will be there in the TRFC shirt I last wore on a sunny day at the Goldstone in August 91, a day when B&HAFC seemed like a 'big' club and Brighton seemed like the best place in the country for a weekend away. We all need to support a team, but let's teach our kids not to hate the others, to have more players and teams they 'like' than 'dislike', to be suspicious of big business and to use their economic power with discretion. VIVA B&HAFC!

Nigel Shaw, a Tranmere Rovers fan

"One week when Plymouth are away I'm going to come up and support your protest. I think it would be a good idea if loads of fans from different clubs turned up at Brighton and joined in. It would show that we're all behind you 100%." This message was posted on the Seagulls Internet web site by Richard Vaughn on December 11. Warren Christmas and Gary Crittenden seized on the idea with all the supporters' groups and Fans United was born. It was a unique day in British football history. Messages of support from fans of 25 English clubs were posted around Hove Park. Fans from almost every league club descended on the Goldstone for the game against Hartlepool United, with Charlton sending the largest single contingent. They were joined by supporters from German and Polish clubs and Albion exiles from New York, Australia, France and the Far East.

It's just like watching Brazil... Five-nil: poor Hartlepool are shell-shocked. "Thanks for one of the best football days of my life." Paul Raymond, Wimbledon. "I have been lucky enough to be at some pretty amazing games over the past few years but Fans United is certainly up there as one of the best. The atmosphere was superb." Sue Rider, Arsenal.

From the high of Fans United to a missed opportunity and farce as Meridian TV broadcast a debate about Albion's problems. The consortium is not represented but Archer is beamed through on a satellite link and Bellotti turns up in the studio with his wife. Key questions are not asked and ex-director John Campbell - the one person who could have embarrassed Archer - is not invited to speak. Bellotti tells everyone that his salary is only £40,000 a year and that no owner of BHAFC has had a penny from the football club. "There is no asset strip."

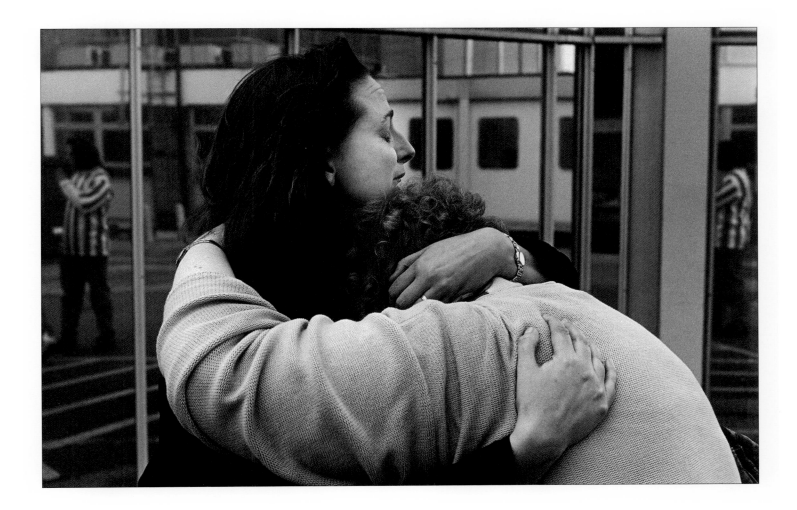

Several fans are overwhelmed by Archer and Bellotti's disregard for the supporters.

Away to Carlisle, Steve Gritt gives encouragement to the players. Another 2-1 loss.

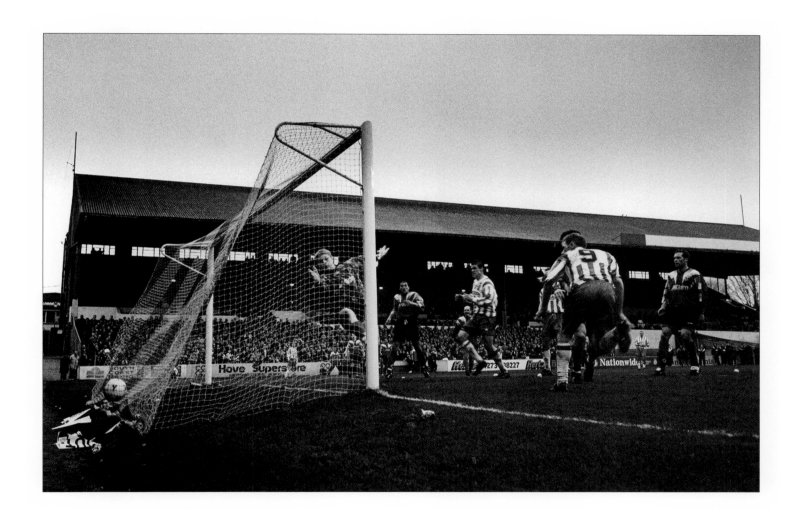

Ian Baird scores in the 74th minute to make it 3-3 at home to Orient. One minute later, Orient score their 4th and madness breaks out as several Albion fans attack Orient players. It is alleged that the players were inciting the North Stand. Five minutes before the end McDonald scores a penalty to end the game 4-4.

The end? 5.40pm Bill Archer with his hands full of trouble leaves the London offices of the Centre for Dispute Resolution. He makes no comment, but CEDR issues a statement: "Following a further day of mediation, the parties are pleased to report that agreement has been reached." Dick Knight emerges at 6.30pm and says, "It's like Albion needing an away win in London and they're leading 1-0 with two minutes to go."

On Friday March 21 at 7.30am Tony Ford, Tony Foster, Callum May and Liz Costa turned their backs on Gillingham's Priestfield Stadium to walk 68 miles back to Hove. The Goldstone Amble will raise funds for the leukaemia ward at the Royal Alexandra Hospital for Sick Children and Albion's Youth Development Fund. Here, Tony Ford changes footwear after 55 miles on Saturday morning. What he didn't say at the time was that he had leukaemia several years ago. Steve Gritt received the Manager of the Month award before the game against Cardiff and by the end of the day the Albion had beaten Cardiff 2-0.

Bad day at Chester. As Bill Archer enters the stadium club historian Tim Carder asks, "When are we going to hear something?" Archer's reply is swift and to the point, "What's it got to do with you?" Chester win 2-1. The ultimate insult is mooning, jeering kids in slow-moving traffic on the way home.

The last evening match ever at the Goldstone is against Barnet. Ian Baird scores as Albion win 1-0.

Waiting for the coach back home and the world is falling apart. A win today at Scunthorpe was vital. The home form had improved dramatically and the gap had narrowed from an 11 point deficit to two points before today's game. The 1-0 loss today had meant that with Hartlepool winning the void was now five points. Only four games left and the next is against promoted Wigan Athletic.

Meeting at the Concorde Bar. Present are Dick Knight, Martin Perry, Bob Pinnock, Ivor Caplin, John Baine, Paul Whelch, Paul Samrah, David Davies (FA), David Richbell (CEDR) plus around 250 supporters. Question to David Davies: "What would the severity of the FA's action be if the agreement was not honoured?" He replied: "The response would be instant." David Davies reflects as Ivor Caplin speaks.

The Albion hadn't lost at home for ten matches. Promoted Wigan are playing for the championship. Hartlepool lose and the Seagulls win 1-0 with a header from Craig Maskell. The gap is narrowed to three points.

The away supporters' ticket allocation is immediately sold and 2,273 Albion fans turn out at the Abbey Stadium, Cambridge. An end to an abysmal away record of one win all season is desperately needed. Robbie Reinelt says "catch this" as he scores on 28 minutes to make it 1-1.

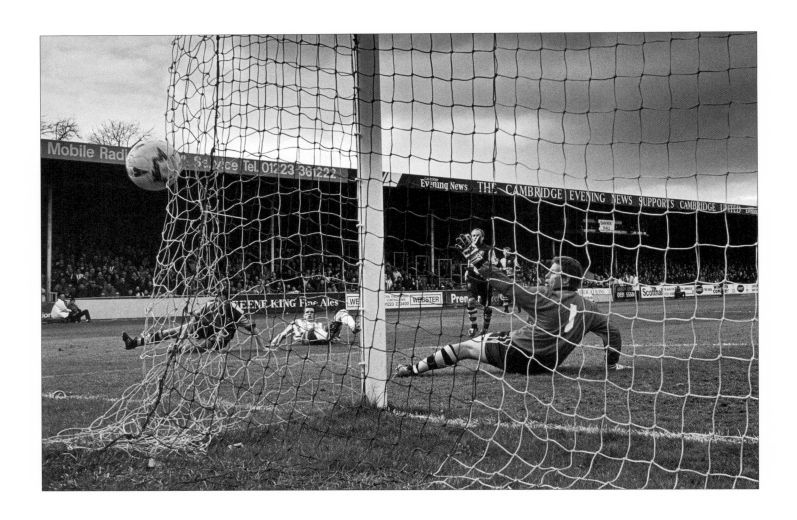

Ten minutes remaining and Storer goes close as Barrett deflects the shot for a corner.

The Albion lay siege to the Cambridge goal and for some it's all too much. The result is a draw. Elsewhere, Hereford drop to 91st position in the league and Albion, three points behind, have them firmly in their sights.

The
DEAL

SLOWLY, painfully, there was a budding of hope in March.

Salvation came much later with the announcement of the restructuring deal on Tuesday, April 22, in the basement of a London hotel. But by early March, Albion supporters were being told that an announcement was imminent, and that Greg Stanley had joined the talks. Stanley's money was keeping the club afloat. Archer, his trustee, could stall no more.

On March 3, John Baine, another future folk hero, told fellow supporters that David Davies of the FA had told him: "If it wasn't for you lot your club would be dead by now." Before the deal was signed there was another spasm of madness at the Goldstone. After Orient's fourth goal in the 4-4 draw on March 8, three Albion supporters ran on to the pitch to attack the celebrating Orient players. It followed a familiar pattern. The actions of a demented few distorting the noble efforts of the many. Ray Wilkins, now of Orient, was knocked over. This time Brighton escaped punishment, but they were lucky.

March 12, and light creeps into darkness. After seven more hours of talks with the CEDR mediators, William Marsh and David Richbell, a deal is agreed but not signed. Over a hundred hours of negotiations have taken place and tens of thousands of pounds been spent. The few details which emerge are mostly encouraging. Andrew Goodall, managing director of Brunswick Developments, who own Brighton Marina, is part of the consortium. The club is negotiating a temporary move to the Coral Greyhound Stadium almost across the road.

Then silence, and a return to the team's ferocious struggle to stay in the Football League. They lose their next three away games to Hull, Chester, Scunthorpe and draw at Cambridge, but win at home against Cardiff, Barnet and Wigan, the league leaders. Strange, inexplicable and infuriating. Survival still seems a long-shot.

The day came, like so many before it, with confusion and swirling rumour. We assembled in the foyer of a London hotel and watched all the main parties in the talks disappear into a backroom. Archer, the invisible man, climbed out of a taxi like a government minister. Eye contact was avoided. The press conference was due to start at 1pm. At 1.20pm we were still waiting. Were they still arguing over the details? Was Archer refusing to sign? For the FA, this was payback time, an opportunity to proclaim the agreement as a triumph for Lancaster Gate. Most supporters, grateful that the club had survived, were too tired to argue.

On the podium, Archer sat next to Knight. When Archer spoke there was a noticeable squirming and shifting of bodies along the row. He referred to "Brighton and Hove Albion DIY" and laughed at his own mistake. His statement was an unintelligible stream of consciousness. When I asked him whether it would have been more honourable for him to stand aside, he said: "I would like to apologise for all the pain I have caused."

No wonder he was being nice. The deal gave the existing owners a 49 and a half per cent stake, the same as the consortium. But Martin Perry of Alfred McAlpine, held the other 1 per cent, which gave overall control to Knight. The vast majority of supporters accepted it, but still sang: "Archer out". Some things will never be forgiven.

The other details: The new owners would submit a planning application within three months for a new 15,000-seat stadium, rising to 25,000 seats. The purpose of the mediation, as laid down by the FA, was that, "professional football should continue to be played in Brighton and Hove and that the future of this historic club should be assured."

A supporters' representative would be added to the new board which would also include Sir John Smith, former deputy commissioner of the Metropolitan Police, and Richard Faulkner, vice-chairman of the Football Trust. Things had been so bad under Archer and Bellotti, people joked, that they had to put a policeman on the board to maintain order.

The club was pallid and bruised and dog-tired of conflict. But rising, rising, towards the final conflict in Hereford.

As fans celebrate, Simon Valder waits to be sentenced at Hove Magistrates Court for making threatening and abusive phone calls to David Bellotti. He had no previous convictions and was expected to receive a fine and a warning. His dependent mother collapsed as a custodial sentence of eight months was given. Meanwhile, Gillingham chairman Paul Scally stated that the Archer/Bellotti deal to share next season at Priestfield was "written in stone" and that he was looking forward to receiving the first down payment of the £300,000 agreement.

Dick Knight chats to Steve Gritt before meeting the players at the training ground.

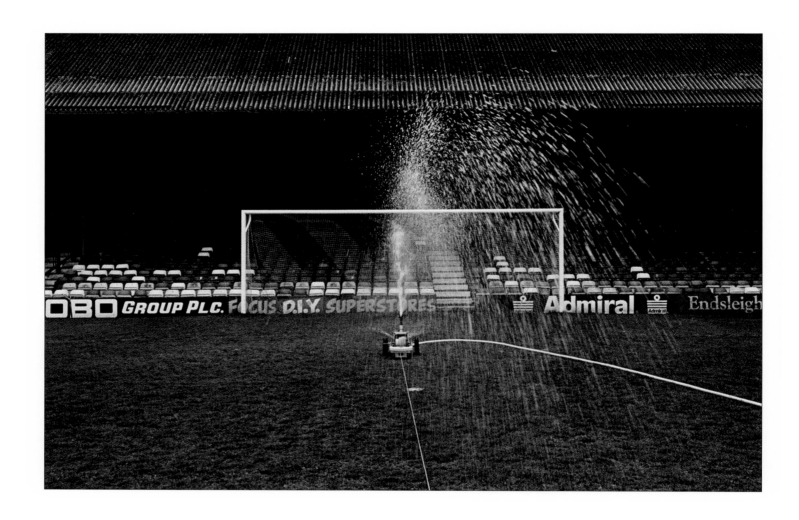

The Goldstone is watered for the last time. Tomorrow will see the most important game ever at the ground. If Hereford win at Orient and Albion draw or lose against Doncaster, relegation to the Vauxhall Conference will be a fact.

Before the game in Old Shoreham Road. The mood is tense although off-the-field developments have raised spirits.

Caught in two moods: the North Stand celebrates Dick Knight's appearance in the ground and prepares to bid farewell to an old friend.

Dick Knight (centre) waves from the directors' box, the first time it's been full for months.

A wreath lays on Albion's dugout.

The Last Post begins and the fans are silent for two minutes. As Liz Fleet plays, supporters remember their best and worst times at the Goldstone.

The team applaud the fans who had played a major part in recent home successes.

Let the game begin...

Half-time and no one has scored. Ian Baird was sent off with Doncaster's Darren Moore on 18 minutes. No news from Orient. Yet.

Minton fires in a corner, Humphreys crashes the ball against the bar and it rebounds to Storer...

Perhaps the most important - and certainly the last - goal ever scored at the Goldstone: Storer volleys into the net.

Happy faces in the South Stand as the North Stand sing. The song is called '2-0 to the Orient'.

After an eternity of added time, the final whistle goes on 95 years of tradition.

One last pitch invasion.

Mixed emotions. Supporters get their own piece of the ground or just stand speechless.

Turf and chairs are the favourite.

Many just stand, reluctant to leave. A draw at Hereford will guarantee safety.

A young couple find sanctuary in the North West corner.

The aftermath. The West Stand seats lay silent.

Goodbye
GOLDSTONE

STEVE Gritt spoke from the bowels of a mine. The one Brighton were climbing out of and the one above our heads in the West Stand. The clanging, thumping sound of the ground being dismantled accompanied the final press conference at the Goldstone Ground, 1902-1997. RIP.

But it didn't rest in peace, and nobody could really blame the fans for that. Many of us wanted to leave it the way we found it, when our fathers took us to watch Brighton in our vanished idealised childhoods. Most wanted a tombstone to take home - a chunk of turf for the garden or the back of a wooden seat bearing a sacred number. Albion fans genuflected at the Goldstone and then smashed it up. Better them, maybe, than Chartwell's bulldozers. The Goldstone lives on - in the back gardens and on the sideboards of its departed family.

It was the morning after that brought the joy. Rushing downstairs to pick up the Sunday papers to see that the line had moved. In Division Three Brighton had been below the salt since October 5. Now somebody else was under it. Hereford, Brighton's final opponents of the season, also had 46 points but had scored three fewer goals. With the 1-0 win over Doncaster, Brighton had lost their home and their heritage and come off the bottom all in one day. The crowd was 11,341.

My ticketless brother-in-law brought his climbing gear to shin up a tree. At the back of the North Stand we passed friends begging for tickets in the rain. We passed them like ghosts, shuffling forward to sort out our own toy chests full of memories and say goodbye to the Goldstone - nursery and, these past two seasons, torture chamber as well.

One-nil to the Albion. A goal from Stuart Storer. A bouquet on top of the home dug-out, the Last Post sounding faintly, a two-minute silence and the Doncaster players with a banner saying: "Rovers players salute Albion fans". Best of all, friendly faces in the directors' box: Dick Knight, Martin Perry and Ivor Caplin, soon to be Labour MP for Hove. It was a place to bring your own children again, not a battle zone. For one final day, at least.

It was a throwback, a footballing Woodstock, an eruption of the kind of beleagured fraternal spirit which supporters of Premier League clubs may never know. When the whistle blew, a tide of soaked and blue-and-white striped humanity raced on to the pitch, to grab their own lump of grass or salute the players making their own perilous way into the directors' box. It was a liberation and a bereavement in one.

Inside, Steve Gritt was explaining why he took the job. "I'd rather take something like this than be sat indoors," he said. "I did say when I came in I'd get the place buzzing again."

"When my dad first brought me to this ground 50 years ago I never dreamt I'd end up as chairman," said Knight. The clanking and banging continued until all that was left was a broken concrete shell and flowers and scarves on a muddy centre circle.

Brighton supporters filed off into the rain, winners and losers on the same day. Some clutched lumps of the Goldstone, some cried and couldn't look back. The Goldstone is gone, history. A new and better one must rise in its place.

Groundsman Ray Archer prepares the penalty spot on the morning of the most important game ever for both Hereford United and Brighton & Hove Albion.

Uninvited and not wanted. David Bellotti arrives at Edgar Street with his wife Jo. He is barracked by both Brighton and Hereford fans.
Hereford United, West Mercia Police and the Football League all asked him to stay away.

Hereford fans feel the strain with nothing less than a win required.

Hereford's goalkeeper leaps for joy as Albion player Kerry Mayo deflects a shot into his own goal. 1-0 to Hereford.

Hereford are playing well and their fans know it.

A dire first-half performance and Albion fans can smell the scent of relegation and the Vauxhall Conference.

Robbie Reinelt picks up the ball, runs through the defence and plants the ball where it belongs. 1-1.

Sussex hears the goal over the radio and Brighton's travelling army of 3,300 fans - plus a few hundred outside - go hysterical.

After enduring 28 minutes of a draw that would be good enough for league survival, John Jackson and Steve Gritt let rip as the whistle goes.
Hereford United sit and stand in silent desperation.

Down and out. Hereford are pipped at the post. Albion endured life in the basement for 203 days. Hereford felt the pressure for just seven days.

Players celebrate as if they have just won the league, not survived it.

Roars from the bath.

When Steve Gritt took the job he had 11 points to make up. He said then that he would be happy if Brighton went into the last game of the season with a chance of survival. They did, and it's going to be the best journey home for a very long time.

A COLLEAGUE sent me a note, only half-joking: "Steve Gritt should get a knighthood." At Edgar Street at 4.50pm on May 3, the 'puppet' came out from behind the counter. He walked on to the pitch in an Albion shirt to salute the 3,300 travelling fans and make what sense he could in the post-match interviews.

Brighton were saved, their supporters in tumult and a new chairman was on the pitch with Gritt, the sorcerer. Nobody had wanted him to come to Brighton. Now nobody wanted him to leave. Knight was promising better times for a club that had been tracked for a year by undertakers. The mark of the old regime remained. David Bellotti, still chief executive on the season's final day, had ignored a request from Hereford not to attend the match.

Brighton's triumph was not Bellotti's, nor Archer's. The supporters celebrated as if let out of a dungeon after 14 years. All the club had achieved was finishing 91st rather than 92nd in the Football League, yet this was unquestionably Brighton's finest day. It was the stuff, perversely, of civic receptions and open-topped bus rides.

At the other end, Hereford supporters were frozen in grief on the low terraces, their heads bowed, their legs unable to function. In the Merton Stand, they sobbed and clutched their faces. It was time to remember that Hereford supporters had made the long journey south for Fans United, to show solidarity among the damned.

Relegation, despair, anonymity was the future that Brighton escaped. Against Hereford they were awful, no escaping that. At the end of the first-half they could have been 3-0 behind. An own goal from Kerry Mayo in a decade of own goals was taking them down to the Vauxhall Conference. And Smith must score? He did in the end. But by then his name was Robbie Reinelt.

Pandemonium, a breaking of the emotional bank, crushing relief for those who felt they would fold under the strain of watching Brighton suffocate. There was nothing to be said, or nothing that made any sense. Brighton supporters embraced and gave each other doe-eyed looks like round-the-world sailors back on dry land. Then the convoy home for a night of the wildest happiness. A Labour landslide and Brighton staying up, all in three days. There was a sense that night that change had broken through at last.

The nadir was reached and passed in the winter of discontent, 1996. Those who are indifferent to Brighton's plight or football generally will never understand how deeply feelings ran. Brighton and Hove Albion FC survived because the supporters wanted it to, and never stopped fighting, and because Steve Gritt and Dick Knight walked into the most blighted club in the land and made it a better, more civilised place to be.

Football historians will look back on the Brighton saga as the model for all resistance movements.

The hate and rage that coursed through the Goldstone is buried with the old stands, and may it never come again.

The bonfire is gone now. The Seagull rises on the breeze.

A last visit to the Goldstone. Malcolm Jupp from Portslade removes turf for his back garden. He talks about the good old days. "Remember when Deano scored that free kick against Ipswich to get us into the play-offs against Millwall?" The Goldstone is dead.

The Archer-inspired Chartwell wrecking crew has arrived. As the bulldozers and concrete crunchers eat up the ground I stand on the pitch which by now is a 15-foot high wave of soil and grass. Focusing on the floodlights, a homeless seagull flies by. For thousands of people the Goldstone is now nothing more than a memory. STEWART WEIR

The POSTSCRIPT

EDGAR Street was supposed to be day one of Brighton's new life. It wasn't. The cheery convoy rode home to Sussex through egg-box hills, but not towards a happy summer in which Albion supporters could lazily scan the papers for news of fresh signings, or the promised utopian stadium that would replace the Goldstone (rubble and mud, now).

The FA's press conference to announce the takeover deal took place on April 22. Three months and two days later Brighton faced a motion to expel them from the Football League. At the lowest point, the club had no ground, no ground-share, no sponsor, half a team and possibly no place in the professional game.

Seven players returned from the summer break out of contract. A storm had blown up over the proposed new stadium complex at Waterhall off the A27 bypass. The club was being run from an office in central Brighton with one phone. No sign of a new High Street shop, and no sign of Archer honouring his promise to cede overall control of the club to the Knight consortium and Martin Perry.

Knight brokered a new sponsorship deal with Donatello, a chain of Italian restaurants. Archer cancelled it. David Bellotti was still chief executive. Knight was working to secure a ground-sharing arrangement with Millwall but Archer was sticking with Gillingham. Many of us believed the club would be kicked out of the League, who insisted, despite the club's protestations, that a £500,000 bond promised by the board had not been paid.

While the two sides argued, the new season was getting suffocatingly close.

The bond was lodged, the motion defeated. Another great escape. After a four-minute count the League chairmen had voted 47-17 to allow Brighton to stay in Division Three. The intention was to open the new season at Gillingham and then move to Millwall after a few games. Later the League ruled that out. Gillingham it was.

"I have put in £500,000 for the bond," said Archer after the meeting. He also repeated his promise to stand down as chairman. "And I intend to add another £1.5m to help take the club into the new millennium."

We'll see.

28 JULY 1997